THE BEST AND HEALTHY FOODS FOR YOUR DOG

INTRODUCTION

This topic is incredibly close to and expensive to my heart. Food medical aid and food drugs ar completely 2 of my passions. It's what I ask my patients concerning each single day.

There ar several foods that truly offer specific advantages for your dog's health. These ar foods which will terribly simply be another to your dog's diet, despite what reasonably diet you feed.

The nice issue is, despite wherever individuals Pine Tree Stateasure} once they come back to me, and betting on their openness to ever-changing the diet, if they're not utterly able to move from kibble to raw (which is my final goal), there ar some terribly basic items they will raise the diet which will build an incredible distinction to their dog's health.

History of drugs = Food
"Let food be thy drugs and drugs be thy food."

– Hippocrates (The Father of Medicine)

Food is age recent drugs. Modern day, typical drugs has strayed quite an bit from this within the last century roughly, however fortunately it's creating a comeback.

Historically, in school, and even for human physicians, we have a tendency to don't get abundant nutritionary coaching the least bit. abundant of the coaching vets do get is proscribed and should even be biased. this can be why heaps of veterinarians don't extremely specialize in it.

But that doesn't mean nutrition isn't necessary …

"When diet is wrong, drugs is of no use. once diet is correct, drugs is of no want."

Food medical care

Nutrition very is that the foundation of health. It's the body's fuel and provides the building blocks for the upkeep of health, tissue repair and energy.

That's why most holistic health practitioners focus an excellent deal on diet and biological process supplements.

No matter what my patients return to Maine for, despite what the priority is, one amongst the primary things we tend to bring up is diet and biological process health.

We need to be wondering about food because the most vital drugs we tend to take each day. Feeding contemporary, wholesome, low processed or unprocessed nutrition is predominant in maintaining your dog's health.

9 Healthy Foods For Dogs To Support Health And Promote Healing

These are a number of the foods I like to recommend for my patients. As a general rule, these are tremendous things that may be another to virtually any diet for dogs.

1. Bone Broth

Bone broth provides such tremendous advantages for your dog. It's virtually a healing drink.

What is bone broth exactly? It's bones, simmered low for many days with apple vinegar. This slowly breaks down all of those nutrients, creating them extraordinarily bioavailable to the body.

Benefits of bone broth:

Improves digestion and helps heal "leaky gut" – All illness starts within the gut (autoimmune, allergies, asthma, chronic inflammation)! Gelatin soothes and repairs the tissue layer lining to assist seal the gut barrier, which may become broken and permit toxins into the blood. Gelatin assists the breakdown of proteins and fats from food, creating them easier to digest.

Assists in detoxing the liver – Glycine could be a powerful precursor for the assembly of glutathione, a strong detoxifier. The liver is such a hard-working organ – it will tons for the body. It's most significant job is to detoxify those things that our dogs are exposed to so the body has got to clear. It flushes out chemicals, hormones and waste. It conjointly provides minerals, acids and electrolytes that boost the hospital ward method.

Reduces inflammation – Glycine and amino alkanoic acid are powerful anti-inflammatories.

Alleviates joint pain – Recent studies show that the parts of bone broth will offer relief from joint pain.

Strengthens bones, joints, muscles, tendons and ligaments – Glycine is very important for building muscle strength. It forestalls the breakdown of proteins in muscle tissue and preserves it (which helps prevent atrophy in aging dogs). The albuminoid contains amino alkanoic acid, glucosamine and chondroitin that support gristle and cushion the joints.

Provides minerals and will increase their absorption – Bone broth is made in macro-minerals (calcium and phosphorus) and trace minerals (magnesium and zinc). Bone broth helps with the absorption of those minerals.

Boosts the system – offers the body tools to spice up inhibitor activity that helps to fight infections.

Improves skin health – albuminoid builds robust skin and protects the skin from aging.

Supports brain perform – Glycine is a vital neurochemical within the brain. Bone broth helps improve psychological feature and memory and promotes higher sleep.

You can build your own bone broth or go from several specialty pet stores.

2. Raw Goat Milk

Raw milk (unpasteurized) is one amongst the foremost nutrient-rich foods around. simply take a glance at the nutrient profile:

Fat soluble vitamins A, D and K2
Healthy fats: Medium Chain Triglycerides (MCT) and Omega-3s
Probiotics and biological process enzymes
Protein/amino acids
Immunoglobulins
Minerals and electrolytes: Ca, magnesium, potassium

There are several health advantages of milk. It's been shown to strengthen the system and scale back allergies. Because of the probiotics and biological process enzymes it's nice for gut health. It will even facilitate repair of leaky gut and promote higher skin health.

What concerning cow milk? whereas there are several factors in cow milk that i favor, I like goat milk. Goat milk is:

Less substance – lower in milk sugar content
Easier to digest and absorb as a result of the fat globules area unit smaller
Higher levels of MCTs (30-35% in goat milk vs 15-20% in cow milk)
Higher levels of anti ophthalmic factor, atomic number 30 and Se
In general, I like to recommend ¼ cup per day for tiny dogs, ½ cup per day for medium dogs and ¾ cup per day for giant dogs. begin out with smaller amounts and exercise to those amounts.

3. Organ Meats

No matter what you feed, be it business raw, do-it-yourself meals or one thing else, organ meat could be a crucial element of the diet. Several business diets and residential cooks can follow the 80-10-10 rule (meaning eightieth muscle meat, 100 percent bone and 100 percent organ meats), however I prefer it a small amount.

Organs and glands are nutrient dense. This includes the liver, kidneys, adrenal glands, pancreas, brain, abdomen (tripe) and heart. Liver and alternative organ meats are unit strength builders (also called blood builders). In ancient Chinese medication they're known as blood tonics. and that we understand that carnivores rate the organs – they are going for the organs initially.

Here area unit a number of the organ meats that you simply ought to try and embody in your dog's diet:

Liver: axerophthol, B, iron, folate, zinc, amino acids, polymer. analysis shows it's nice for building strength and endurance
Kidney: axerophthol, B12, riboflavin, iron
Heart: CoQ10, B-complex vitamin, amino acids, collagen
Adrenal glands: vitamin C
Brain: omega-3 fatty acid, selenium, zinc, B-complex vitamin
Tripe (green, not bleached): biological process enzymes, probiotics, selenium, zinc, B-complex vitamin
**Try to urge organ meats from organic, pasture-raised animals.

4. Eggs
Eggs area unit thought-about an organic process powerhouse. They've been known as the foremost complete macromolecule and are actually 100 percent bioavailable. And they're very easy to add to your dog's diet.

They provide:

High quality macromolecule and amino acids
Vitamins A, D, E advanced B vitamins

Omega-3s
Antioxidants
Calcium, selenium, zinc
One of the items the egg area unit most helpful for is vessel health, thus don't place the plug of the previous few decades that say eggs aren't smart for your heart! The cholesterol in eggs really regulates cholesterol within the body. and therefore the brain and liver swear heavily on cholesterin for traditional operation. They're conjointly smart for eye and skin health.

Try to realize free vary eggs. Cage-free isn't an equivalent as unconfined thus search carefully!) Free vary eggs have double the maximum amount of omega-3 fatty acid, three times additional fat-soluble vitamins, seven times additional carotene, hour additional axerophthol and area unit ninety eight less doubtless to hold salmonella!

Raw eggs are a unit fine. For an outsized dog, AN egg daily is nice ANd for smaller dogs associate with perhaps [*fr1] an egg. Or, associate with each alternative day – no matter what causes you to snug.

5. omega-3 fatty acid Oils
For omega-3 fatty acid oils, I like to recommend feeding little, oily fish on a daily basis.

There area unit several health advantages to the current including:

Brain food
Anti-inflammatory
Joint support
Kidney perform
Heart health
Skin and eye health
Sardines and anchovies, as terribly little fish, haven't had time to accumulate the toxins found in larger fish. They're cleaner and provide a tremendous supply of omega-3s. And keep one's eyes off from farm-raised fish.

Oily fish is wealthy, therefore begin with smaller amounts initially and work your high. For smaller dogs, you'll be able to begin with ½ a sardine per day, and for larger dogs exercise to the maximum amount as a tin each different day.

Other sources of omega-3 fatty acid oils:

Krill oil – very bioavailable, however it's over-fished therefore it's not nice for the surroundings
Calamari oil – this has the very best concentration of DHA and Environmental Protection Agency and it's the foremost property with the smallest amount negative impact

6. MCT Oil
One of the opposite medicative power foods that i prefer to suggest for all of my patients is MCT oil. MCT stands for medium-chain lipid, an awfully sensible fat. It's thermally stable, therefore it doesn't promptly oxidize, even with high heat. that produces it nice to cook with.

There area unit a massive array of health benefits:

Brain food – improves psychological feature and helps decrease insanity
Anti-microbial (bacteria and yeast/candida) – saturated fatty acid
Full of antioxidants and minerals
Reduces inflammation
Boosts system health
Good for skin and oral health
As a healthy fat, it conjointly helps to fight cancer. one in every of the items we all know regarding cancer cells is that they can't use fats. Cancer cells want aldohexose, or sugars, that carbs break down into, to fuel themselves. we are able to facilitate starve cancer by providing a diet that contains additional healthy fats and fewer carbohydrates.

Make sure you get MCT oil that doesn't have saturated fatty acid. Most dogs love the style. A general suggested daily dose is regarding one tsp per 10-20lbs of weight. begin slowly and work your high to it.

7. Kelp

One of the explanations brown algae is thus smart for dogs is that it's packed with trace minerals. Our thusils are getting so depleted that they're mineral deficient, thus we want to appear for alternative sources of trace minerals. The ocean is providing these minerals. It's the lifeblood of the world.

Kelp algae absorbs heaps of its nutrients in its fronds/leaves, not from the roots. Compared to plants that grow onto land, ocean vegetables have 10-20 times additional vitamins, minerals and amino acids. It's conjointly a robust supply of trace minerals and complicated phytonutrients.

Some of the minerals that are made in brown algae are iodine, selenium, metal and Mg. There area unit many health advantages of those nutrients, including:

Thyroid health
Metabolic health

Nervous system health
Digestive system health
Immune perform
8. Mushrooms
Mushrooms are unit one in all my favorite foods which will be offered on each day. I take advantage of them myself each day. Mushrooms contain a number of the foremost distinctive and potent natural medicines in the world. They've been employed in Chinese seasoning formulas for hundreds of years as a result of supplying such powerful health advantages.

Some of the simplest mushrooms include:

Turkey Tail
Reishi
Cordyceps
Lion's Mane
Shitake
Chaga
Maitake

Medicinal mushrooms are packed with vitamins and nutrients as well as beta glucans, flavonoids, prebiotics, organic process enzymes and antioxidants. One of the foremost well-known advantages is the wonderful boost to the system. Organic process health and anti-cancer advantages are smart reasons to include them in your dog's diet.

9. hard Foods

Fermented foods area unit an incredible supply of helpful bacterium (probiotics). they sometimes contain a wider selection than supplemental probiotics with a lot of focused numbers of bacterium. They're additionally nice for supporting immune functions. hard foods assist in detoxing the viscus and chelates significant metals/chemicals, will facilitate heal leaky gut and IBD.

One of the explanations hard foods area unit therefore awe-inspiring is attributable to all the nutrients. The fermentation method produces:

Vitamin C, Godwin Austen and B vitamins
Acetylcholine – a neurochemical
Choline – balances and nourishes the blood
Enzymes support digestion and metabolic activity
Lactic Acid – represses cancer cells
Some of the simplest choices for hard foods are:

Kefir

Yogurt
Fermented veggies
Fermented fish stock
Fermented fish sauce
Kombucha
To feed hard foods, physical exertion to one tsp per 10lbs of weight per day.

CONCLUSION

Hope this book helps a lot?
It's very important to keep our dog healthy,start giving your dog all these food mentioned above.

-

www.ingramcontent.com/pod-product-compliance
Lightning Source LLC
La Vergne TN
LVHW020547160826
845677LV00015B/4249

* 9 7 9 8 3 5 2 1 7 2 1 2 4 *